CHOICES!

Published 2020: Golden Child Promotions
Publishing Ltd

Portland House,

Belmont Business Park,

Durham,

DH1 1TW

goldenchildpromotionspublishing.gold

Read This First! Download *Why I Know That You Do Not Love Your Children!* Ebook FREE!

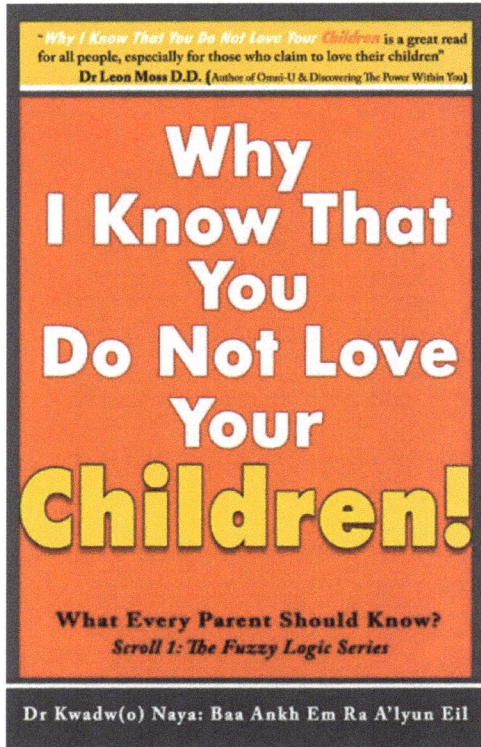

Just to say thanks for reading my book, I would like to give you a free e-book! ($6.99 Value)

https://BookHip.com/JFWKZB

CONTENTS

—◆—

INTRODUCTION

———•◆•———

I've decided to write a book today.

As I look around the world, nothing makes sense anymore, not to me anyway. I can only see two trains of thought, and I've decided to spend some time sharing my mind with you.

Well, I might be crazy, I might not, please let me know your thoughts.

My name is Baa Ankh Em Rayay.

No! No!! No!!! I don't even know my name!

My name is Kwadw(o), my name is...

Kwadw(o) Naya: Baa Ankh Em Re A'lyun Eil.

That is not even my name yet, but it's my name-to-be, this is the new me and it's a new start.

Anyway, let's begin.

CHAPTER ONE
NEW TIMES

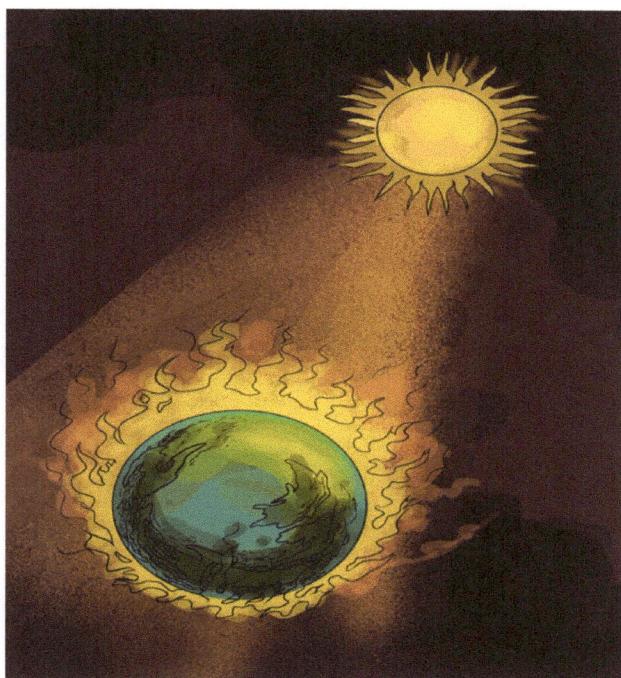

Kwadw(o) Naya: Baa Ankh Em Re A'lyun Eil

It is known that we have transitioned into a new cycle: the sun cycle, going from the age of Pisces into the age of Aquarius (some would call it the Information Age). For the next, 6000 years or just under, it's going to be very hot, hotter than it's ever been before because our planet is getting closer to the sun. I think this all started in the year 2000.

There are still going to be a lot of changes and I feel that already, some changes will be good while some will be bad. It's high time people made a choice. I've made mine and I'm going to tell you more about this in chapter two.

But honestly, I just wanted to speak about this topic – *"The New Times"*–and address it from what might be a new angle. Everyone is entitled to their own opinion, so it's perfectly fine if you think I'm crazy.

CHAPTER TWO
TRANSHUMANISM

"They have found the science of Transhumanism.. So, they won't need humans anymore. And they can live forever. It's crazy." - Malik Khan

Looking around, I see two trains of thought: there are two main paths. People are being led to follow one blindly, while others' open their eyes to another path and act to follow it instead.

As I said earlier, my name is Kwadw(o) Naya: Baa Ankh Em Re A'lyun Eil, and I would like to talk about my family. We grew up on a farm. We believed, and still do believe, in natural living, growing our own crops, vegetables, fruits, and so on. We don't really believe in tablets and medicine; these pills and potions just don't make sense to us. We know about natural healing. Tablets and medicines are just a replication of nature. Why mess around with an imitation when you have the real thing?

Choices

We would rather go out there and take the real substance but as I say, there are two trains of thought. Some, like me, subscribe to the opinion of living in accordance with nature. Granted, technology is good. Honestly, I love technology, but not more than I should. It should complement natural experiences and resources but not replace them.

The other school of thought that many of us have been led towards is transhumanism. Surprisingly, many people are looking forward to human enhancement through technology, replacing our natural bodies with artificial parts.

For instance, Elon Musk, the multi-billionaire, is a huge supporter of transhumanism. He has spoken on the subject often and has made some great moves. I've heard him speaking about putting chips in peoples' heads and claiming that they will enhance thinking ability. It seems he's really keen on that, on anything that will make the future better and brighter for himself, or the human race entirely.

As I said earlier, everyone is entitled to their own opinion. Elon Musk can look forward to this day all he wants, but as for me, I'll stick to nature. There is nothing wrong in taking a bit of monatomic gold; I'd prefer to do that than have a chip in my head any day.

After all, we all have chips anyway but that's a different story. Well, some of us do. Some of us have bank cards, mobile phones, and other bits of technology.

Chip! Chip!! Chip!!!

CHAPTER THREE
ROBOTS

The robots are going to take our jobs one day.

No! The robots are already taking our jobs. Think about who serves you when you go to the bank. It's no longer a member of the staff, is it? Instead, they advise us to use a machine. Machines can help us, but more often than not, people are waiting to see people that are not actually people. Just more machines.

It's the same problem in supermarkets! No people, mostly machines. We have robots everywhere. You wait in the queue and you have robots asking you what service you require or encouraging you to self-scan your shopping. You have to call the robots first, before you can speak to a real person. Sometimes, you have to even leave a message with a robot.

This is actually too much for me, maybe because I'm a traditional guy.

I'm full of love. I like to deal with people, not with machines, but like I said, it is each to their own.

Robots will be driving cars soon. Oh! It's happened already. Did you hear about what happened when they were testing a driverless car? A driverless car actually ran over someone and killed them. Then they tried to sue the Uber driver for negligence; who was in the vehicle to oversee the technology, not to drive the car. Why was that person in there? Shouldn't a driverless car be without a driver?

All I'm trying to say is that there are a lot of different people on this planet. We all are different animals, different human animals. I think there are about three to four different types. But we all come from different cultures. So, in this respect, I can only speak about my own culture, about my own family, about our values, because they are all I know. You might say me and mine are simple, but we believe in nature and we value it. We believe in growth. We believe in evolution. We believe in love. We like to deal with real people.

When I was younger, I used to listen to a lot of music. I used to feel free. But today, everything feels more restrictive. Driving down the street thirty years ago, there were no speed cameras and most of the car doors weren't even locked. But now, don't even think about it. We have speed cameras, dashboard cameras, alarms, and immobilisers. Technology over technology, tracks this and tracks that. We are not even safe on our mobile phones or laptops! The internet administrators and chieftains are tracking our every move, watching our internet habits and tailoring advertising at every step! Technology is policing our culture, at this point, it might be our culture. It might be the people's culture who have been running things for a long time or who have the money and power to make the influences, which is all well and good, but it's not our culture.

Of course, it's a no-brainer that technology is good. We love technology and we see it as a doctor that can help us evolve. But my family only uses technology in a way that actually supports nature. We humans are from nature; we are from the ground; we are from the dust. We can hold our hands up to our mouth and feel the breath of life. I don't think a computer will ever be able to do this. Granted, it might be able to replicate or copy some certain mannerisms or maybe connotations, but there are always going to be glitches. A computer will never replace the human next to us completely. That's how I feel. But who am I?

CHAPTER FOUR
PEOPLE

Kwadw(o) Naya: Baa Ankh Em Re A'lyun Eil

What is wrong with people these days? Have you noticed how many people are no longer genuine? Have I been surrounding myself with the wrong people? I don't know. I spent all my life living in England, half living in London and the other half living in a small town called Darlington, in the northeast of England, not far from Newcastle.

Though I've visited many other countries on holiday, I'm using England as the metrics to measure by. From this, I've noticed that most people these days do not seem to be genuine. Many have hidden agendas. They might smile to your face or shake your hand, while talking about you behind your back or ridiculing you. I don't get this at all. I find it hard to comprehend this type of behavior. It certainly isn't how I was brought up. It's not how I am. I'm really genuine. I try my best to like everybody and to love everybody. I don't like to be anywhere where I'm not welcome. If I feel that the environment is not warm or conducive, then I take myself away, even if it is from family.

Sometimes, I've felt more comfortable with my enemies than with my 'so-called' friends and family. You might think otherwise but I have observed people's ulterior motives, and I don't like it. You might not agree with me, but I would love to hear your thoughts. I will leave my email address; your thoughts would be very much appreciated.

CHAPTER FIVE
RELATIONSHIPS

Choices

I can speak on this with confidence. Relationships are not what they used to be. And that is sad. I don't know what it's like in your country, but in England, I've personally seen the difference. It might just be that I am in a bad place with some really bad people. Feel free to correct me if I am wrong.

I'm just saying how I see it. This is just a quick book to show that I can share my thoughts, interact, and basically introduce myself to the world. I will be writing a few books; I have got quite a lot of interesting stuff to say. But this time, I just want to engage and discuss with you. And as I said, I am sharing my mind and my observations, wondering if they are the same as yours.

I love my grandparents dearly; they have been together all their lives. Wonderful generation!

Kwadw(o) Naya: Baa Ankh Em Re A'lyun Eil

They brought up big families with great integrity, good morals, who all lived with honor, respect, and most of all, love. That's what I remember. I remember my grandma used to come around from Birmingham, and she would come and cook cornmeal porridge. I used to love it. My uncles and my aunties, all of us used to be together whether it was in Birmingham or Darlington. It was very, very nice.

Moving on to my parents... they tried. They were together for about 16 years. Then they split up for some time, remarried, they are still remarried. They did quite well, but they did not last as long as my grandparents did. As you can see, relationships are losing their longevity. We move forward one generation, and a lifetime was cut down to around 16 years.

Choices

I'm 43 years old, I have two younger sisters, one is 40, the other in her late 30s. We all have the same relationship history. Single most of our lives, maybe a few short-term relationships here and there. I found it really, really hard to be in a relationship. When I was 39, I decided I wasn't going to play ball anymore; enough is enough. I want to be serious. I said to myself, I'm going to find a nice woman, get married, and settle down.

I decided to start a relationship with a lady I was introduced to for the purpose of marriage. The lady lived in Ghana and I lived in England. I liked her and I gave the relationship three years to flourish. I put a lot into it; I invested time, money, energy, and everything. In fact, I really settled down and was a good boy for nearly three good years. When maybe in the past I had not been too good but because of her, I became a good boy. I worked really hard to put things in place. I even planned to move to Ghana and settle down with her early next year. But at the end of the three years, what happened? Everything was gone! Just at the click of a finger, the lady ended our relationship.

And just when it gets to the point when everything was coming to fruition, boom, I get a kick in the face, I don't want to elaborate much more but we both know what happened.

I invested heavily in this relationship, not just financially but emotionally. Even to this day, I still have a driver's license in Ghana I have money in the bank but look at me, what did I get? What went so wrong? I don't like things that are not transparent. I believe in love; I believe in truth. I would never end a relationship in a day. Relationships are for life!

It seems to me that some values have been lost in the world. What do you think? Do you agree or disagree? I welcome you to give me your thoughts.

Now, let's talk about my sisters' experiences. They're great women and they are still single. It's not that they don't want to marry or settle down. They are trying to find good quality gentlemen, they have tried a few relationships, but they haven't had success because quality gentlemen are nowhere to be seen. Well, every one of them showed himself as the opposite. Now we are all in our late 30s and early 40s, we haven't settled down yet, we haven't even met the person we will marry, which I think is very sad.

What is going on in the world? Surely, my sisters and I aren't the only ones having this problem? Or is this a common story around the world? I don't know what it's like in your country, I've never lived in your country, but here in England, we have a lot of single mothers claiming benefits. Some of them have up to six children with different fathers. And unfortunately, our government is set up in a way that empowers the woman and discredits the man. And the woman might think, 'Hey, we don't need no man!' Blah, blah, blah. They have power and they want to be independent.

Is this working, if you look at the big picture? You might be one of those women who doesn't depend on a man and you might think it's a great thing. And you might think, 'You are crazy!' 'What are you talking about?' 'Things are better for us now'. But, me personally, I believe in family, I believe in love, I believe in happiness,

and I believe in music. Those are just my
thoughts. I'm sorry if I sound crazy.

CHAPTER SIX
LIFE

Choices

What is life? Are you happy with your life? Can I ask you that? Do you like what you do? Oh, I see. Most people's life revolves around two things. The main thing in life should be love. But you see, too many people have been taken away from nature, from themselves. Too many of us have been put in too small a box, with too many restrictions. Some would call it the matrix.

People put labels on everything. But what I know what I see, what I feel, what I hear, what I sense, what I touch, what I taste, and everything to do with my senses. People can say whatever they like, but we always remember how they made us feel.

So, are you happy with your life? What is it you do? Are you happy with what you do? Some people don't work, they are unemployed and don't do anything. These are the useless eaters of the world. Some people are happy with that, some are not. Others work for money; they work very hard for money and are very proud. Still some work very hard and don't get paid a lot, and they're not happy.

The general consensus is that most people work; they spend sixty to eighty hours per week, like robots, they work, work, work. What they don't realize is that they are just being used like batteries, servicing other people's operations. And then when the batteries run out, they are just replaced by somebody else. Nice!

And then there's a business owner, of some Jack and Jill shop, she or he or even she and he have got this little business working sixty to eighty hours a week and making some decent successes along the line. But this work takes up so much of their life, that they barely have any time. Their lives are hardly any different.

26

Choices

I want to talk about two things; time and money. People spend their time gaining money, too much time. I can't say that everybody does it, but many people chase money. Just you talking to them wastes their time. They're all trapped in the illusion. They think they have their own plans, but really it belongs to someone else. Don't be disturbed, there's a new way now.

The system is not working, it needs to be ripped up. You go to school, get a good education, and find a good job. Or you go into further education, you finish your studies, then you go out to get a job. More like you waste a lot of time and money on education and you can't get the job that you want. You got chewed up in the system. And then before you know it, you're working in a job that you don't necessarily like or enjoy until you are seventy and you can retire.

Kwadw(o) Naya: Baa Ankh Em Re A'lyun Eil

At seventy that's when you start living your life, it's finally your time. But the only thing is you just don't have the money. Everything that you have worked hard for is not yours, it's not for you. You learn that only after you retire. Too late! I think the best solution is for families to get together and make something, do business like they did in the past. The system encourages everyone to go out and be an eagle in this world. We need to free ourselves from these constraints. We really need to grow and evolve.

How we think about money is really important, because money is not real. It's a piece of paper. It's a tool. We need to speak about it. We only have time, time for ourselves, time for our family. We don't need to be speeding through because we need money. If this carries on, I think I will go to Africa, buy a big plot of land, turn it into a farm, and grow everything I need to be self-sufficient.

We don't even need to pay for electric; we can have solar power, water power, and wind power. So, we don't need to fall for these games anymore. But these are just my thoughts. Who am I to say this? You might not agree but I just felt like sharing them with you. I love you all.

CHAPTER SEVEN
GOD & RELIGION

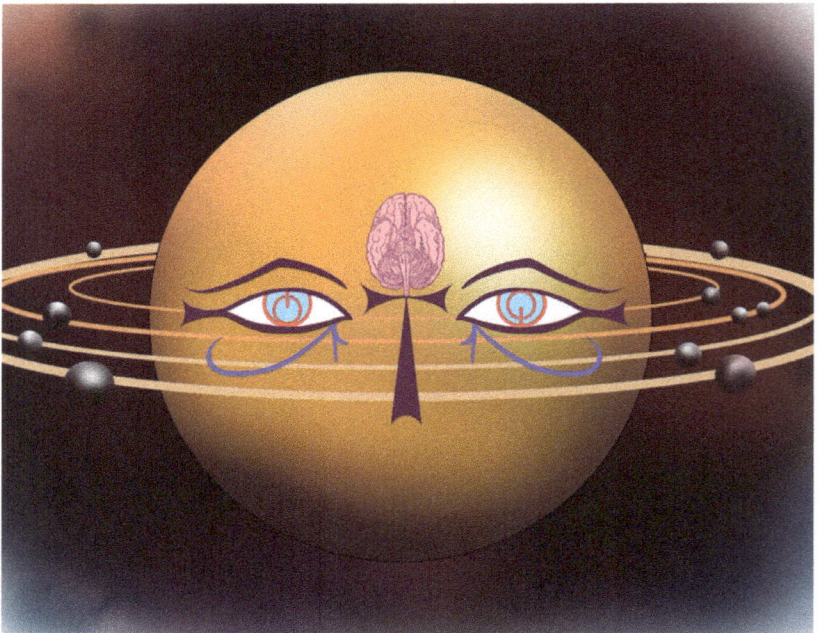

Choices

I think that it's only fair to talk about God and religion, even if I don't particularly want to address this topic. In this life, there are so many people, so many mindsets, so many different cultures, and so many beliefs. That is where I feel the problem lies: beliefs. What do you believe? Do you know why I ask that? *Because if you believe, you don't know.*

Have you ever heard the saying; knowledge is power? I've heard it too many times. And I know it's true. They say that seeing is believing. Some people will believe something only if they see proof. Do you know the makeup of the eye and how it operates?

I MY-SELF, cannot just BELIEVE something because it is the WAY that I have been TAUGHT or LED to BELIEVE.

Kwadw(o) Naya: Baa Ankh Em Re A'lyun Eil

If one BE-LIE-VES they obviously don't KNOW, that is all I have to say.

"A belief is a poor substitute for experience" - Tony Robbins

Everything we see is a reflection and is reversed. I suggest that the next time you look in a mirror, you look up mirror image. Why do things look the way they do? Well because of the *eye technology*.

Religion will lie to you. All I'm trying to say here is that we are all equal, but we are all different, (unique in our own right). **WE** are all **ONE** and we **ALL** are a part of **THE ALL** (EL KULUWM). We all have different mindsets, different cultures, different perspectives, and different views. And I think this is great; we should always be appreciative of other people's views of life. It's each to their own.

Choices

Every man and woman should do his or her best to become what that they would like to be, whether negative or positive. Obviously, I like to dwell on the positive side. But I do realize that, in order for everything to coincide on this plane or this PLAN-E.T., we need to have balance. So good and bad must coexist. But there's no such thing as good and bad as it is down to personal perception. That is a topic for another day.

Let us just refer to it as positive and negative for now.

CHAPTER EIGHT
TECHNOLOGY VS NATURE

Choices

What comes next? **Choices.** We all need to make them; we need to decide on the life we would like to live. Would we like to live? Or would we like to do something different? Maybe, you need to reflect on this for yourself. Who knows? But to me, it's an obvious choice. And we all need to make that choice wisely.

I don't really like to say that one of the options is inherently good or bad. It is magnetism; like attracts like, positive people stick together, and negative people stick together. I would like us to focus on the two main choices. If you sit back and look at the world around you, it's nature or transhumanism.

The people who've been running the planet for a long time, their time is over now, and I'm not sure if they know. I do think they tried to run things the way they felt was best. They brought technology, thinking that it would help lead humans to a better existence, but as for me personally, I believe that it is not leading us but is causing us to digress.

A friend of mine lives in America; he is a very good guy, he spends a lot of time saying nice things, spreading good knowledge, and teaching people. Of course, the establishment doesn't like him; I don't know why. About two to three days ago, Today is the second of August 2019, the police followed him, pulled him out of his car, and harassed him. He's not new to this, he recorded the police while they pulled him out of his car. They severely roughed him up and treat him really bad. They even smashed his phone. I have the video; please check out the link or footnote so you can see for yourself.[1] Statistics state that in his country the same police force has killed approximately 156 people this year.

Shouldn't we be able to say that technology has made life easier, or has it regressed our very being? Just see for yourself. When this man was arrested, they smashed his phone and held him in a cell all night. He was unable to contact friends or family, because he relied so heavily on technology, he didn't know any phone number. Years back, we used to naturally learn everybody's phone number as we had to manually dial them. It seems technology has made life easier but that hasn't come without cost; our very beings have regressed.

---

1   https://www.facebook.com/lamel131/videos/1825238024288862/UzpfSTU1MTU0NDQ1ODoxMDE1NzY3Njg0Nzk1NDQ1OQ/ accessed 2nd August 2019

On a positive note, at least he did have the ability to actually record what was going on. But they didn't like it, they destroyed that technology, but their own was working against them. They didn't like it. I'll just say that the choice is quite simple. Technology or nature. Obviously, we will always have technology and we'll always have nature.

As long as I'm on this planet, I'm not going to let these people do away with nature. It makes no sense. I like to see green grass and not concrete; that's me though, you might like concrete. That being said, that's why I don't like England. It's filled with too much grey and too many high-rise flats.

When I was in London, I was an estate agent. The houses in London are very expensive, and sometimes many families share one. Five to seven people in one room, paying high rent. And most of these people come from Africa, the Caribbean or European countries like Romania where they have large amounts of land back home. As in nature, they grew their own crops, planted their plants, and reared large livestock. Now they work for money and live in a box on land. They then spend up to thirty-five years paying for a house on a mortgage. Let's break down the word mortgage: 'mort' / 'gage', 'mort' – 'gage', M-O-R-T, you don't pay till your mort.

Let's break down the word mortgage: 'mort' / 'gage', 'mort' – 'gage', MORTGAGE = DEATH PLEDGE: Latin words Mort-Gage, literally translated, **Mort** means (Death), **Gage** means Pledge), "Debt Slavery = Human Mortgages = Debt till Death!

Time to rethink I FEEL, there MUST be a better way than this?

I see the children today; the millennial children, they love smartphones, apps, and technology. I like to dabble now and again but I don't like to keep my mind too busy with the distractions.

I like tools that make things easier, like technology that makes communication quicker, for example. But you need to appreciate the use and the purpose of every single item. That's what I feel. Are we using technology, or is technology using us? I think that's what we need to have a look at, especially as parents for our children; we should go to nature.

How many things are natural? When we go to the supermarket and buy an apple, is it a real apple? Or is it genetically modified? If you buy a melon, is it a real melon? Or is it genetically modified? Are these all prepackaged fruit breeds? I don't like people playing with my food. But people are doing it and it's all being approved by the Food and Drug Administration.

How is this so?

And what about all the preservatives that are used in preserving our foods?

It feels weird and strange watching fruit that never goes off, don't you think?

All in the name of profit.

CHAPTER NINE
HIGH TIMES

Choices

I can't really spend time worrying about all of you guys, or maybe I should say, I can't really spend my time worrying about all of you ladies and gentlemen. But I will never leave you out. So, if I see something that will help you or help the world to be a better place, I will always share it with you.

I'm actually going through a process at the moment; a process of taking myself away from all the negativity surrounding me and away from anything or anybody that is draining my energy. I need to keep my battery fully charged at all times. At this moment, I spend a lot of time alone. I have friends, good friends. Not all of them live near me, many live in different countries, but they are all normal people, good people. Unfortunately, a lot of these people are not my family. The family is not what they used to be.

Just yesterday, I spoke with my grandson for the first time in over a year. There have been some complications in the family, which I will address in my other books. He asked me why we don't get together anymore. He said, 'Granddad, do you remember that time, do you remember that Easter, when all the family was together?' His step mum, his aunty, his great-grandma, his great-granddad, his grandad... most, if not all of his family were all together (which is a rarity). It was really nice! And then the following year, half of the family were missing. I wasn't there and many other people weren't either. And he said to me, 'Granddad, it was nice when all the family were together... I really enjoyed that', and then he compared it to the year after, when there weren't many family members around, and he sounded really sad. Guess what? The poor boy is not even seven! Yet, he realized that for more than a year, maybe two years the family have not been together.

When I speak, most of my family members think I'm crazy. They said they don't want to hear that. All they want to do is have their nice time, looking good, spending money, basically following a system, or let me say, supporting a system that is not working anymore. The system that hasn't worked for a long time. And when Kwadw(o) or let's say Mr. Baa mentions this to these people, his good friends and family, they don't want him around, he immediately becomes a pain in the ass. They'll say he's afraid, he's like a headache, a stupid person, a killjoy.

CONCLUSION

———◆———

I've made my decision, a decision I made a long time ago. I'll be gone soon. I am moving to Africa. To live with nature, hopefully to find a wife or two, have many children, settle down, have a large family, and enjoy the sunshine and my life. I just thought that I would share with you a little bit of my mind, it's been a pleasure. I hope I haven't upset you too much. And thank you for your time. And if you have any questions or you would like to give me any feedback, even if you don't like what I'm saying, it would be

Choices

very nice to hear from you. I will leave my email
at the end.

Thank you.

AFTERWORD

———◆———

I just thought that I would write this book today. Although; I really didn't know what I was going to say, I didn't even write it. The secret is: I've actually spoken this book into an app that turns it into text. I just wanted to try to write a book like this. I've heard that many people are doing this, so I thought I'd try it myself. So, now I've done it! I've written a book in just one day.

I started it over an hour ago and now I'm looking at the app, I've got loads of words on the screen. Some words have been written in good English. Some words I need to decipher and put together. Some of it has gone a little bit higgledy-piggledy, but it has made the process a little bit easier and quicker. I'm not sure if I prefer this way, but I thought I would just give it a try and see how it works. Now, obviously, I will have to work out how to get the words out of this app into a document so I can edit it and get back to you ladies and gentlemen.

Well just as I've said, it's been a pleasure once again. I hope you've enjoyed what I have spoken about. I hope I haven't upset you too much. I look forward to seeing you all and speaking to you in the future and please look out for my other works. I've got a lot of good material coming out soon. It's in progress, a lot of deep and interesting things, which I'd like to discuss with you and raise awareness of, though a lot of it might be new to you.

Kwadw(o) Naya: Baa Ankh Em Re A'lyun Eil

It's been a pleasure once again. I love you all. Please take care. Stay safe. And hopefully, we'll speak again. Thank you.

If you feel to leave me a review online, it would be greatly appreciated :9)

Kwadw(o) Naya: Baa Ankh Em Re A'lyun Eil

onlygold@goldenchildpromotionspublishing.gold

Please look out for Choices 2

Choices

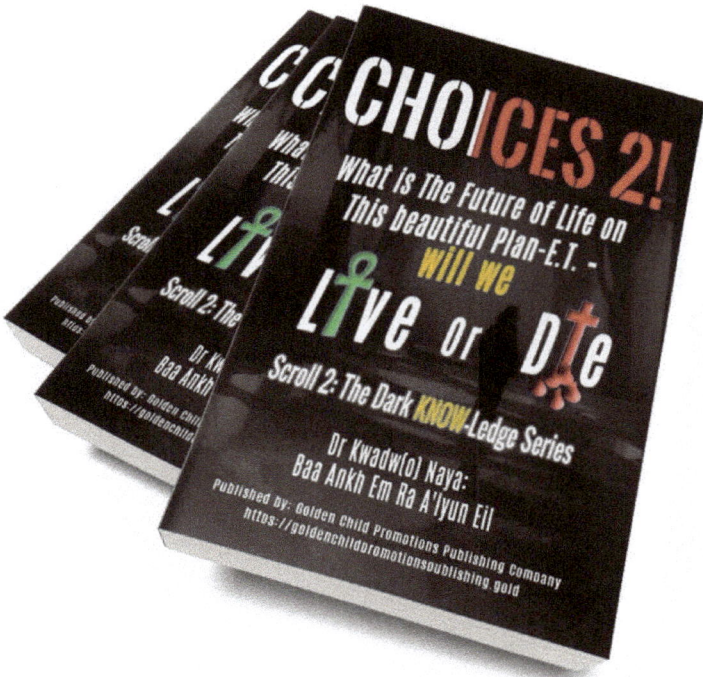

You can order your copy here for only

$3.77

https://goldenchildpromotionsp
ublishing.gold/product/choices2
-live-or-die-scroll2/

ACKNOWLEDGMENTS

Acknowledgment and thanks to Hayley and aspivey5 for the editing. Thanks also to mogumash for assisting with the illustrations, Steven at Expert Designs for dealing with the transcription, João Cabral from Pexels for the book cover background image, and a big thanks to hansbarrow who kindly took care of the book cover and formatting. Your help is truly appreciated.

ABOUT THE AUTHOR

———◆———

Kwadw(o) Naya: Baa Ankh Em Re A'lyun Eil

Born: Catterick Garrison, UK

Nationality: British

Race: Autochthonous Carbonite

Genre: Non-Fiction

Notable awards: A Masters in Business as well as many other vocational qualifications.

Kwadw(o) Naya: Baa Ankh Em Re A'lyun Eil is an Author, Director, Mentor and Life Coach ('Transformational'), he is a new gentleman on the scene, one of the most promising newcomers for 2019.

He was born in a country where he has never been accepted, raised in a broken poverty-stricken home, which he was thrown out at the age of 15 never to return. Surprisingly he has had a very good career, NOT GREAT, and is educated to master's level with 'degrees' in street knowledge. Despite his successes there has always been some unseen FORCES working against him, which he is only too happy to share.

Somehow, he has excelled with everything that he has touched and is not afraid of CHANGE, moving from running his own estate agency in the capital city of London (UK) to becoming a fully established author, mentor and life coach.

Choices

Kwadw(o) Naya: Baa Ankh Em Re A'lyun Eil is ready to share his KNOWLEDGE, WISDOM, and OVERSTANDING with YOU ALL.

He has written 25 books to date, please watch out for his works.